Water from Air: Water-Harvesting Machines

by Cherese Cartlidge

NORWOOD **H**OUSE **P**RESS

Norwood House Press
PO Box 316598
Chicago, Illinois 60631

For information regarding Norwood House Press, please visit our Web site at:

www.norwoodhousepress.com or call 866-565-2900.

© 2009 by Norwood House Press.

LIBRARY OF CONGRESS CATALOGING-IN-PUBLICATION DATA

Cartlidge, Cherese.
 Water from air : water-harvesting machines / by Cherese Cartlidge.
  p. cm. — (A great idea)
 Summary: "Describes the invention and development of water-harvesting machines. Includes glossary, websites, and bibliography for further reading" —Provided by publisher.
 Includes bibliographical references and index.
 ISBN-13: 978-1-59953-196-0 (library edition : alk. paper)
 ISBN-10: 1-59953-196-8 (library edition : alk. paper)
  1. Dew harvesting—Juvenile literature. 2. Water vapor, Atmospheric—Juvenile literature. 3. Basic needs—Juvenile literature. 4. Water supply—Juvenile literature. I. Title.
 TD415.C37 2008
 628.1—dc22

                                          2008010780

Manufactured in the United States of America.

Contents

Note: Words that are **bolded** in the text are defined in the glossary on page 43.

Chapter 1

The Need for Water

Clean water is one of the most precious resources on Earth. In the United States, most people take clean water for granted. They twist the handle of a faucet or push the button on a water fountain and cool, safe water comes rushing out. This is not always the case in poorer countries.

For example, in El Salvador, a small country in Central America, clean water is sometimes hard to find. Four-year-old Elisabeth drank water from the well in her village. But the water in the well wasn't safe. It had **parasites** in it. Parasites can make people sick. You cannot see or smell them; for most people there is no way to tell whether their water is safe or not. Elisabeth almost died after drinking the water from her well.

Elisabeth lives in the village of Milagro a Dios. An earthquake struck there in

A woman fills a bucket with water from a polluted well. Lack of clean water is a problem in many poor countries.

to buy bottled water, so they kept using the unclean well water.

Drinking or cooking with unclean water is a problem for much of the world. It can cause **diarrhea** and **typhoid fever**. It can even lead to death. Each year between 5 million and 9 million people die from drinking unsafe water. Today more than 1 billion people around the world don't have safe water. And experts think that number will continue to grow. This book looks at the many causes of this problem and explores some of the solutions, including a machine that "harvests" water from the air.

2001. The earthquake caused **sewage** to spill into the village's water supply. This is how the well water became **polluted**. Elisabeth's family didn't have money

Children collect water from a well in Zimbabwe. In 2008, the country declared a national emergency over a cholera epidemic caused in part by a clean water shortage.

Causes of Unsafe Water

Human beings take the water they need from nature. However, sometimes nature "takes it back." For example, when an area goes too long without enough rain, it is called a drought. Severe droughts can last for many years. Drought leaves little water for crops, livestock, and humans. The result may be hunger and disease. During times of drought, it is difficult to grow food. Also, animals die. This makes the food shortage worse. Meanwhile, whatever water people are able to find is used mainly for drinking and cooking instead of washing or bathing. This causes germs to spread and leads to an increase in diseases.

That is what happened in Somalia, a country in northeast Africa, in 2005. A drought began there that year. Only 18 percent of the people had safe water to drink. There wasn't enough water to wash with. And there wasn't enough water to get rid of sewage. This led to an outbreak of diarrhea and **cholera**.

Other natural disasters can lead to a lack of safe water, too. These include earthquakes, hurricanes, and **tsunamis**. In 2007 Kenya, also in Africa, was hit by several floods. In some areas flood waters swept sewage into the water supply. This led to an outbreak of deadly cholera.

Cholera

Drinking unclean water can lead to many diseases. One of the most serious is cholera. This disease can cause violent diarrhea. It can also cause vomiting and muscle cramps. People with cholera lose a lot of body fluids and salts. They may feel very thirsty. Their bodies may stop pumping blood. People can die from the disease in only a few hours.

Cholera is caused by **bacteria**. People get the disease from food or water that has the bacteria in it. Sometimes sewage gets into places that store drinking water. This can lead to an outbreak of the disease. The best way to prevent cholera is to make sure people have safe water to drink.

Getting Safe Water

Safe drinking water is the number one need after a natural disaster. One way to meet this need is to bring in bottled water. Sometimes, though, it is very hard to get bottled water to people in need. Hurricane Katrina in 2005 was one of the deadliest storms in U.S. history. Thousands of people's homes were ruined by the floodwaters. Groups such as the Red Cross and the Federal Emergency Management Agency (FEMA) that respond to disasters weren't able to come right away. And because floodwaters were up to 20 feet (6m) deep in places, many streets and roads were gone. It was days before help arrived. During that time thousands of people had to go without food or safe drinking water.

Water-Harvesting Machines

When people need fresh, clean water in a hurry—and getting it to them is difficult or impossible—it can be pulled right out of the air. The machines that do this are called water harvesters. Different water harvesters work in different ways. But they all are designed to turn the moisture in the air into water that is safe for humans to drink.

How much water is in the air? More than you might think. Have you ever set a can of cold soda down on a warm day? Within a few seconds, beads of water begin to collect on the can. Within a few minutes, you might even see a small puddle forming at the base of the can. That water is not coming from the can—it was in the air that came in *contact* with the can. The can was cold enough to make the air surrounding it reach its **dew point**. Assuming the can is clean, that water is safe to drink!

Did You Know?

There are rules to make sure your tap water and the bottled water you buy in stores is safe to drink. The government's rules make sure it is clean and free of parasites.

Imagine a water harvester large enough to create hundreds of gallons of water a day. It could be driven to the location of a disaster like Hurricane Katrina. One group that uses water harvesters in this way is the Red Cross. The Red Cross is an international **relief organization**. It provides help to people in need all over the world. This includes victims of natural as well as man-made disasters such as wars. The Red Cross uses water harvesters in several nations. It has sent them to parts of Africa and Asia.

The Red Cross also sent several to Sri Lanka after a deadly tsunami struck in 2004. Huge waves crashed ashore after an undersea earthquake. Within seconds floodwaters began to rise inside buildings. People scrambled to escape. Some of them had to swim out of

Huge bags filled with clean water await delivery to victims of Hurricane Katrina in 2005.

windows. About 2.5 million people lost their homes. Millions more were unable to find food or drinking water. So the Red Cross sent several water harvesters to help provide safe water.

These water harvesters are about the size of a tractor trailer. The amount of water they can make depends on how much moisture is in the air. These machines can make about 265 gallons (1,000L) of drinkable water a day. This is enough water to meet the minimum needs for drinking, cooking, and bathing for about 33 people a day. There are smaller machines, too. The smaller ones look a little like a water cooler. These machines can make between 2 to 10 gallons (8 to 38 L) of water a day. Water harvesters of this size are meant for household or office

To be ready at a moment's notice, a Red Cross worker loads a water-harvesting machine for transport.

Humans Need Water

Why do we need water? It doesn't have any nutrients or calories, but we need it to stay alive. Our bodies depend on water. Water helps digest food. It helps remove waste products. And it helps the blood travel all through the body.

Some animals, such as camels, can store water in their bodies. Humans cannot do that. We need to take in water each day. Some experts say the average woman needs to drink eight glasses of water each day. And the average man needs twelve. Without enough water the body becomes **dehydrated**. Severe dehydration can cause the body to shut down and lead to death.

use. But after a disaster, they could provide enough emergency drinking water for up to three or four people a day.

How Water Harvesters Work

The air we breathe is made up of nitrogen, oxygen, and small amounts of other gases. It also contains water vapor. The amount of water in the air depends on the weather. For example, the air contains more moisture when it's raining. During a drought the air contains very little moisture. The amount of water in the air also depends on the part of the world you're

Did You Know?

Your body has more water in it than bones. That's because your body is about 60 to 70 percent water!

in. In desert regions, there's very little moisture in the air.

Most water harvesters work by pulling air through filters. These filters trap dust and other **impurities** in the air. The water that's in the air condenses, or beads up, on the filter. This water drips from the filter and is collected. Then it is exposed to ultraviolet (UV) light. UV light kills germs and bacteria and makes the water safe to drink. The machines used by the Red Cross can make about 10 gallons of water in an hour.

Although these water harvesters have been used successfully in some parts of the world, they have a few drawbacks. They only work in places with a lot of moisture in the air. They don't work in very dry places, such as deserts. And some of them only work well in certain **temperatures**. Most water harvesters need a temperature of 65°F (18°C) or higher to work well. Also, it takes a lot of energy to keep them working.

Boiling Water: The Good and the Bad

In some parts of the world, such as parts of Africa, people must boil their water. This kills bacteria and parasites in the water. And it makes the water safe to drink. But boiling water can cause other problems. Some people do not have money for fuel to boil their water. They end up burning wood instead. Using wood to boil water can lead to deforestation, or cutting down too many trees. Burning the wood also pollutes the air. And it takes a lot of time to gather the wood and boil the water. This can make life more difficult for people who are already struggling just to survive.

A Better Way

One man thought he could come up with a better water harvester. His name is Abe Sher. Sher knew of the problems in getting water to people after Hurricane Katrina and other recent storms. He also knew about the problems of getting water to people in deserts and during droughts.

Sher decided to make a different kind of water harvester. He wanted a machine that would work even in very dry places. He wanted it to work well no matter what the temperature was outside. That way, people who really needed water could get it. And it wouldn't matter where they were or what caused the water shortage.

Abe Sher

Abe Sher began his career as a lawyer in Los Angeles. But he also held a degree in business administration. He turned to business early in his career. He started a number of companies around the country. Sher's companies did well. So he decided to put his knowledge and experience to work in a new area. He decided to help solve the problem of getting clean drinking water to people in need. In 2004 he founded a new company called Aqua Sciences. This company is based in Florida.

Abe Sher, shown here after meeting with FEMA officials, wanted to make a water harvester that would work in very dry climates.

Chapter 2

Water from Thin Air

A simple salt shaker sparked the idea for Abe Sher's new water harvester.

Salt is what got Abe Sher thinking about a water-harvesting machine. He thought back to his grandmother's salt shakers. He remembered how the grains of salt stuck together, or clumped, on **humid** days. This happened because salt absorbs water from the air. Sher's grandmother put rice in her salt shakers. The rice acted like a sponge. Rice is full of pores, or tiny openings.

These pores absorbed the water from the salt and kept it from clumping.

Sher thought about the salt in the shakers. He thought about how salt absorbs moisture from the air. Why couldn't he use salt to pull, or harvest, water from the air? He decided to try. One day he left some ordinary table salt out on a counter. The salt absorbed moisture from the air and clumped up. Sher knew salt was the key to a new type of water harvester.

A New Technology

In 2004 Sher started a new company called Aqua Sciences. The company created a water harvester called the Emergency Water Station based on Sher's ideas about salt. The Aqua Sciences machine was different from earlier machines. It took water from the air in a way that had not been done before. It did not pull the air through an air filter. Instead, it used a totally new technology.

The technology used by Aqua Sciences relied on a very salty liquid. The air was forced through this liquid. The salty liquid

Desiccants

The salty liquid in Aqua Sciences' machine is known as a desiccant. This is a material that acts as a drying agent. The white beads inside the little paper packets that come in a shoebox or in a new purse, for example, are desiccants. The beads draw water out of the air and help keep the shoes or the purse dry. And the salt used in Aqua Sciences' machine draws water out of the air much like these beads.

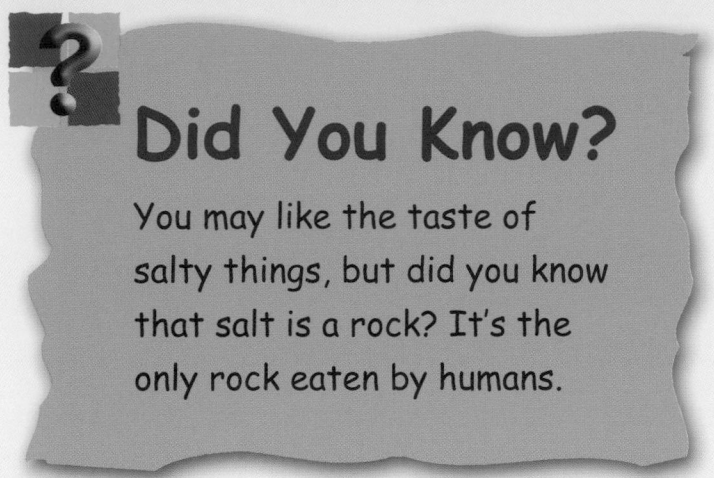

What It Can Do

The water harvester made by Aqua Sciences can make about 1,200 gallons (4,542L) of drinkable water a day. That's enough to supply about 150 people a day with safe water for drinking, cooking, and washing.

The water is put into plastic pouches inside the water harvester. These pouches

A 20-foot water harvester, made by Aqua Sciences, stands at the ready for use by FEMA in a disaster area.

drew water out of the air just like the salt in a salt shaker. As Sher said to a reporter, "[The salty liquid] actually rips the water molecules from the air." The salt also acted as a natural cleaner to help kill germs in the water. The water was then removed from the salty liquid. This was done with heat and chemicals. A filter cleaned the water of any remaining germs. This made the water safe to drink.

are stronger than plastic or glass jugs. And the water stays fresh longer because the plastic blocks sunlight and resists the growth of germs. The pouches are placed in cardboard cartons for storage. Each pouch has a spout on the side. This spout can be opened to dispense the water.

The Aqua Sciences water-harvesting machine looks like the back half of a tractor trailer—the long truck you might see driving down the highway. It can be easy to move, and it can be taken almost anywhere. It runs on electricity. If there is no electric power, it can run on electricity made by a **generator**.

You may wonder if water that was pulled from the air and put through a salty liquid would taste okay. In fact, water harvested from the air tastes just like any other water—it's no different from tap water or bottled water.

It Works Almost Anywhere

The most important feature of the Aqua Sciences water harvester is its ability to work even in places with little moisture in the air. The amount of moisture that's in the air is called humidity. Humidity is

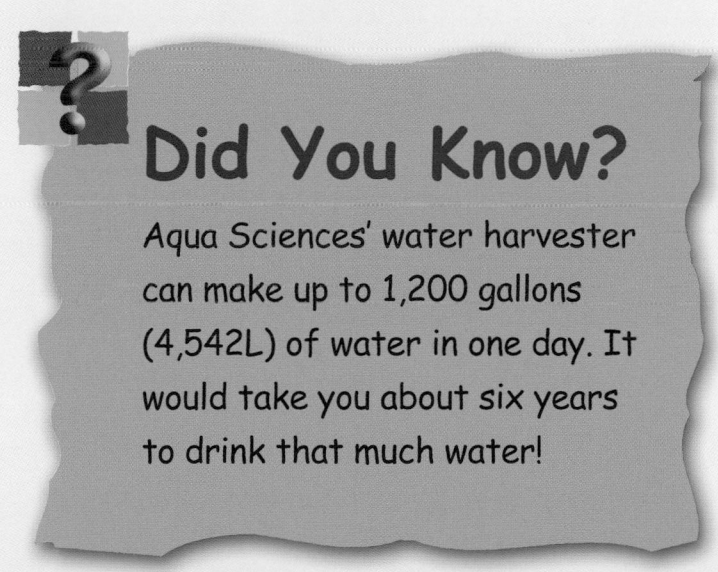

Did You Know?

Aqua Sciences' water harvester can make up to 1,200 gallons (4,542L) of water in one day. It would take you about six years to drink that much water!

After getting clean water from a water harvester, these women carry the jugs back to their village.

given as a percentage. So, for example, if it's raining outside, the humidity would be about 99 or 100 percent. In a desert region with little moisture in the air, the humidity can be lower than 20 percent. All of the early water harvesters needed a high level of humidity in order to work. Most needed 70 percent humidity. Even the larger machine used by the Red Cross needs at least 55 percent humidity.

The Aqua Sciences machine will work in places with very little moisture in the air. It will work in humidity as low as 14 percent. This means it will work in a desert. It can also produce water from the air no matter what the temperature is. No other water-harvesting machine in the world worked under the same conditions as the Aqua Sciences machine.

The Aqua Sciences water-harvesting machine's ability to work in very dry places is important. It can improve or

The Driest Place

The air around us always contains some moisture. This moisture is in the form of water vapor. Think of a foggy or misty day. At these times you can actually *see* the water vapor in the air. But on sunny, clear days, the moisture is still there, even though you can't see it. How much moisture is in the air depends on the temperature. The air holds more water vapor at higher temperatures. And at lower temperatures, the air holds less vapor. In Antarctica the warmest it gets is a frosty –20°F (–30°C). So it shouldn't surprise you to hear that Antarctica is the driest **continent** on earth. In fact, it is considered a desert. One region in Antarctica has not had rainfall in more than 2 million years!

even save lives in dry areas of the world. The most severe water shortages are often in very dry areas. Australia, the Middle East, and parts of Africa and China have shortages of water due to low rainfall. These are all very dry places that are especially at risk during droughts.

Australia, for example, is the driest continent on Earth, next to Antarctica. A region of Australia had a drought that began in 2002. In 2008, there was still no end in sight. Parts of the country became so dry that the ground cracked. One rice mill in Australia used to process enough rice for 20 million people around the world. But the mill stopped running because rice no longer could grow. The crop failed because of the drought.

Some experts worry that there will be more droughts around the globe in the future. This could lead to more water shortages. Ethiopia is a country in eastern Africa. It is very dry there. It has suffered from drought for many years. Ponds have dried up in many parts of Ethiopia. This has happened near the village of Sabant. The ponds were once a source of drinking water. The people of the village now have little water for themselves. And their cows and camels are dying from lack of water. This means that the people there also have no milk or butter to sell. As a result, they do not have money for food and medicine.

Parts of nearby Kenya are also suffering from the long drought. There, corn crops have failed. Agnes Nundu lives in a small village in eastern Kenya. Her children play in the corn fields. But the fields

African villagers welcome a truck carrying clean water from a harvester site. Water harvesters can provide water even in the driest places.

have turned to dust. Nundu says her children have never seen corn grow.

A water harvester that works in very dry places can be important in countries such as Ethiopia and Kenya. Aqua Sciences' machine can pull drinkable water from the air nearly anywhere in the world. Abe Sher told a reporter that "the atmosphere is a river full of water, even in the desert. It won't work absolutely everywhere, but it works virtually everywhere." This means the company's water-harvesting machine can help people all over the world.

Chapter 3

Changing the World

Water made by a harvester pours out of a tank pipe in Iraq. Trucking in water costs more than making it in a harvester.

The conflict in Iraq gave the United States a special set of problems that water harvesters helped to solve. Iraq is a desert region. People need to drink more water than usual in hot climates in order to keep their bodies healthy. But there is much of Iraq where there is little or no water to be found. Sometimes the only water near the military base was polluted. This meant that water had to be shipped to the bases. The military would have to bring bottled water long distances by truck. At any given time, almost one in three military trucks in Iraq would be carrying water. This is an expensive and dangerous way to get water to soldiers.

Water for U.S. Troops

That is why the U.S. military started using water harvesters in Iraq. The Army already had ways of making small amounts of drinkable water. One way used a small water harvester to pull water from the fumes of a **Humvee**. To do this, the water-harvesting machine is mounted onto the back of the vehicle. It gathers water from fumes that come out of the exhaust pipe. It then filters the water to clean it. This system can make about 1 gallon (3.8L)

of drinking water for every 2 gallons (7.6L) of fuel the Humvee uses.

Tainted Water

One way that water harvesters helped soldiers in Iraq was making sure their water was clean. Unclean water can cause many health problems. That happened at several camps in Iraq from 2004 to 2006. A private company was paid by the military to supply water to the camps. The soldiers had clean bottled water for drinking. But the water they used for everything else was tainted. It had bacteria in it. The bacteria came from raw sewage that was dumped too close to a stream. The water that came from the stream wasn't cleaned well enough to kill all the bacteria. This water was used for cooking, bathing, brushing teeth, and washing clothes. Several soldiers at the camps became ill. Experts believe these problems were caused by the unclean water.

It takes about an hour to clean the water. Soldiers can get their drinking water directly from a tap on the back of the Humvee. Even though the system does not make much water, it is still useful.

But the Army wanted something that would work on a large scale. It needed a good system for dry climates such as Iraq. So in 2004 the U.S. government asked a group of companies to find ways to pull water from the dry Middle East air. It spent millions of dollars to encourage these efforts. Meanwhile, Aqua Sciences came up with its water harvester without money from the government. And in 2006 the Aqua Sciences machine was selected as the best. The government gave the company a contract to supply the military with its new water harvesters.

Since then the military has been using the Aqua Sciences machines to get water to soldiers. The smaller machines can make 600 gallons (2,271L) of water a day. And they can fit in the back of a truck. This means they can follow the soldiers when they are on the move. The larger machines are not as easy to move. But they make more water. They can

Aqua Sciences supplies water to U.S. troops in the Middle East with equipment such as this 40-foot water harvester.

make up to 1,200 gallons (4,542L) of water a day and be parked on military bases. Each makes enough water to meet the minimum needs of about 150 soldiers a day.

Disaster Relief

Soldiers in combat are not the only ones in need of water. In 2004 Florida was hit by four hurricanes. These hurricanes all took place in only six weeks. A tropical storm also struck around this time. Together these storms caused a great deal of damage. Buildings were torn apart. And there was a lot of flooding.

One of these hurricanes was named Charley. After Hurricane Charley, many people got sick. The hurricane had torn holes in sewer lines. Some of the sewage

The Army's Future Combat Systems

The Army's Future Combat Systems (FCS) is a way to make the Army more modern. The program uses the most advanced weapons and equipment available. This includes Aqua Sciences' water harvester. The first FCS brigade will be ready in 2015. But some parts of the program are already being used.

One idea behind the program is for the Army to be able to survive in remote, harsh areas. The program will let the Army train just about anywhere in the world. This means soldiers will be able to train in the actual climates where they will be fighting. That's where the Aqua Sciences machine fits in. Mounted on the back of a tank, it can provide water to soldiers who are training or fighting where water is scarce or is not safe to drink.

spread to the water supply. People who drank the water became ill.

The Federal Emergency Management Agency (FEMA) is a government agency. It helps people to prepare for disasters. It also helps people after disasters have struck. The Florida office of FEMA didn't want to see any more people get sick from bad water. So they bought two water harvesters from Aqua Sciences in 2006.

The FEMA machines produce drinkable water from the air just like the ones used in Iraq. But they differ in several ways. The FEMA machines are able to clean bad water that may be in ponds and wells. Each of the machines in Florida can clean up to 8,000 gallons (30,283L) of water per day.

Each of the FEMA units is in a large steel container. Within each container are nine water-harvesting machines. If one machine fails, the others will keep making water. Each unit also has two generators.

Water harvesters are secured inside truck trailers at a FEMA warehouse. In a disaster, these trailers will be dispatched quickly.

Help for Hospitals

A powerful earthquake shook Singapore in 2006. Thousands of people were injured. In one town, a hospital was destroyed. The other hospitals in the town did not have room for all of the injured. At one point, 2,200 patients awaited care in a hospital that only had 700 beds.

In a disaster like this, medical workers often set up field hospitals for treating injured people. Field hospitals are also used in combat zones. Some water-harvesting machines make hot and cold water. These machines can prove useful in a field hospital. They can provide water for drinking and washing, both of which are needed in hospitals.

could make water for a week by running on the two generators. Also if one generator fails, the second would keep working.

FEMA stores its water harvesters near Orlando. They are on trailers, ready to be moved wherever they are needed at a moment's notice. In the days before Hurri-

Did You Know?

Americans drink 29 billion bottles of water a year. That's more bottled water than any other country in the world. This is in spite of the fact that Americans have the cleanest, most available water in the world.

Hurricanes and other disasters often cause long power failures. The generators let the Aqua Sciences machines keep working even if the power goes out. The FEMA units

cane Ike crashed into the coast of Texas and Louisiana in 2008, many of the people evacuating from the Gulf of Mexico passed these units on the highway. They were headed in the opposite direction—to help the people who did *not* evacuate. In the city of Galveston, Texas, it took many weeks before the water system was repaired and service restored. Until then people had to boil the water.

Cheaper than Bottled Water

The Aqua Sciences machine isn't an inexpensive piece of equipment. FEMA paid about $500,000 for each of its units. But buying bottled water and getting it to people also costs a lot of money. It costs about $15 a gallon to truck in drinking water after a hurricane. With the Aqua Sciences machine, it only costs about 20 cents a gallon. In the long run, Florida's FEMA office believes it is saving money by using these machines.

The U.S. military hopes for the same. Shipping bottled water to soldiers in far-away places costs a lot of money. First it goes by cargo plane. Then it's trucked

This emergency water station can be used during a disaster when clean water is unavailable.

across land to the troops. All of this movement ends up costing about $30 a gallon. But the water-harvesting machine can reduce the cost to about 30 cents a gallon.

Water-harvesting machines can solve one other problem that bottled water cannot. After a while, bacteria can grow in bottled water, making it unsafe. The shelf life of bottled water is about six months.

Did You Know?

A gallon of water weighs more than 8 pounds (3.6kg). If you had to carry around all the water you needed each day, it would weigh about 50 pounds (22.6kg)!

Shelf life refers to how long a food item can be stored and still be safe to eat or drink. Because water harvesters constantly make new, fresh water, large numbers of bottles may no longer have to be stored.

Best Invention

The Aqua Sciences machine was introduced to the world in 2006. So it has not been around very long. But it's already being put to use in a few places in the world. Florida and Iraq are two of the places the water harvester is being used.

In the few short years it has been around, Aqua Sciences has drawn lots of attention. In 2006 *Time* magazine named its water harvester as one of the best inventions of the year. *Time* said that it would be a lifesaver for troops in the desert and disaster victims. And, especially in Iraq, it's already having an important impact on people's lives by providing safe drinking water to troops in the desert.

In 2007 Aqua Sciences got even more praise. Its machine won an award for best new **technology**. The award came from a contest held by a business newspaper, the *Wall Street Journal*. In order to win an award, a product had to be a "breakthrough." It couldn't just be an improvement on technology already in use. Rather, it had to be an important new advance.

The Aqua Sciences machine was such a breakthrough. It can produce thousands of gallons of fresh, clean drinking water from almost anywhere on the planet. This includes places with very little humidity. This has the power to change lives around the world.

Chapter 4

Other Ways to Make Water

Water harvesters are one way to get safe water. But there are several other methods around that let people "harvest" clean drinking water. It's important to have these other methods available because getting enough water to drink is a basic human need. People can survive for several weeks without food. But they'll die within eight to ten days without water. So when it comes to getting enough water, people are willing to try every method available.

That's the case in Beijing, the capital of China. The city suffers from water shortages. So does much of northern China. In this region severe droughts are common. China has tried to find ways to increase rainfall. This is especially true in Beijing. The growing number of people who live there is putting a big demand on the region's water supply.

Dew Harvesting

Early one morning Joseph Cory and Eyal Malka saw droplets of water on a spider's web in the desert. This gave them an idea. Cory and Malka are architects who live in Israel. When they saw the dew on the spider's web, they were inspired to create a dew-harvesting device. Their invention catches dew in a "web" made of canvas. The canvas is stretched out like an upside-down pyramid. The pyramid funnels the dew into a tank below. The tank filters out dirt and germs. This makes the water safe to drink. And it can be used by people in areas where water is scarce.

Cloud Seeding

One idea being used in China is called cloud seeding. This is a method of trying to make clouds rain by filling them with chemicals such as silver iodine. All clouds contain tiny droplets of water. These droplets combine to make bigger drops. If it's cold enough, they freeze into ice crystals. When they get heavy enough, they fall from the clouds. This makes it rain (or snow, if the ice crystals stay frozen). Seeding clouds with chemicals helps to make these droplets of water clump or freeze together. So cloud seeding can cause rain to fall sooner or more often than it normally would.

In Beijing, an old anti-aircraft gun sits on a hill just outside of the city. The gun fires canisters of chemicals into the clouds. Officials fire the canisters into the sky whenever there are clouds. In other areas, airplanes, rocket shells, and anti-aircraft guns seed chemicals into clouds to try to make them rain. Hu Zhijin is a cloud expert

A Chinese soldier prepares to load iodine canisters that will be used to seed clouds.

in China. He says that nearly every time it has rained in northern China, methods such as cloud seeding have been used.

Cloud seeding is also used in around 25 other countries, including Australia, Canada, Russia, and the United States. Utah is one of the driest U.S. states. It uses cloud seeding to help produce rain. In 2008 Utah had four cloud-seeding programs. The state says this method has increased its winter rainfall by 14 to 20 percent.

Desalination

Some say the answer to the world's water problems lies not in the clouds but in the ocean. The Earth's surface is covered with water, but only about 1 percent of it is drinkable. The rest is too salty for people or animals to drink. It's also too salty for growing crops. But it's possible to take the salt out of seawater. This process is known as desalination.

Perth is a city on the western coast of Australia. It is home to 1.7 million people. This region has been in a drought for several years. The government was worried the city would run out of water. So it built a large desalination plant in 2007. This plant turns water from the ocean into drinking water. The plant makes enough water for 20 percent of the city's daily use.

Experts think desalination may be the best hope for getting water to people. There are 13,000 desalination plants in the world. Most are located in North Africa and the Middle East. These areas are very dry, but they are located near

A worker checks equipment at a desalination plant in Israel. Some experts say desalination is the world's best hope for clean water.

oceans. They have an endless supply of salt water that can be turned into freshwater. Saudi Arabia, for instance, gets 70 percent of its water through desalination.

Desalination has some drawbacks. The biggest is that it costs a lot of money. Just building a plant can cost up to $1 billion. Removing salt from seawater also takes a lot of energy. The equipment and energy to run the plant costs much more than many

Harvesting Rainwater

Australia has lots of droughts. Many parts of Australia get so hot and dry that the leaves of trees and plants are scorched. So Australians have started "harvesting" the rain. Barrels or tanks are used to collect the rain. The water is then used to water lawns, wash clothes, and flush toilets. And as long as it's filtered and cleaned, the water can even be used for cooking and drinking. In most Australian states, all new or remodeled buildings must have rainwater tanks installed. Also, people must use only rainwater for watering their lawns or washing their cars. Otherwise they face large fines.

Did You Know?

Humans and other animals can't drink seawater. The only animals that can are saltwater fish because they live in the ocean.

countries can afford. And experts believe that in order for desalination to be a viable answer, each plant would have to be run by its own small nuclear reactor. This would greatly increase the cost of this method.

Reusing Water in Cloudcroft

The city of Cloudcroft, New Mexico has found an answer to its water problems. Cloudcroft is high up in the mountains. That means it can't get water that runs down a mountain, like cities at lower elevations can. And recent droughts have caused water shortages in the city.

So Cloudcroft decided to reuse wastewater. The city is building a plant to clean wastewater and return it to the drinking water supply. Cities in many parts of the world recycle wastewater. They use it to water crops or fight fires. Not many of them use it for drinking. But that may change soon.

Solar Cleaner

Countries in Asia, Africa, and Latin America have a great need for clean, safe, water, even though many have sources of freshwater already. India, for instance, has many rivers. But the rivers are often polluted. The Ganges River is one of the most polluted rivers in the world. But many people who live along the river have no other source of water. So they must drink water from this river. If polluted water in rivers and lakes could be cleaned, these would be good sources of water. Two methods are being tried using the sun to help provide clean water.

One method uses only the heat of the sun to clean water. The process uses clear plastic bottles that range in size from about 1 to 2 quarts (.94L to 1.8L). The bottles are filled with dirty water. Then they are placed in full sunlight for at least six hours. On cloudy days, the bottles must be exposed to the sun's rays for two days straight. The water in the bottles is cleaned in two ways. One is through radiation from the sun's ultraviolet (UV) rays. The other method is through heat. When the water temperature is above 122°F (50°C), the cleaning process works three times faster.

Mary is a woman who lives in Uganda. She used to walk up to 5 miles (8km) a day to find water. And the only water she could find was polluted. She and her children were constantly sick from drinking the bad water. But then a local church showed her how to clean water with the plastic bottles. Since then Mary and her children have been much healthier.

This method is used in other countries in Africa, Asia, and Latin America. It's designed to be used by single households.

Did You Know?

You may already be drinking treated sewage and not even know it. The United States and many other countries dump treated sewage into rivers. These eventually return the water to the supply of drinking water for millions of people.

People only need the plastic bottles in order to have clean, safe water. However, there are some problems with the process. One is that sometimes people do not leave the bottles in the sun long enough. This means their water isn't totally clean before

Special solar panels like this one are used for cleaning water. The water is heated in the panel until it is ready for drinking.

they drink it. Another concern is the plastic bottles themselves. As the plastic gets older or becomes scratched, it allows less of the sun's UV rays to get to the water. This can also lead to people drinking water that's not clean.

Putting Solar Panels to Work

Another way to clean water using sunlight is with solar panels. Water is heated with a solar panel, which collects energy from the sun. The water is kept in the solar panel until its temperature reaches 175°F (79°C). This kills germs and parasites in the water.

This method has been used in 40 countries around the world. These include El Salvador, Guatemala, India, Malaysia, the Philippines, and Tanzania. In one part of Tanzania, doctors are seeing far fewer

Solar water heaters, like this one in France, allow sunlight to help create clean water.

cases of typhoid fever. People in this area are using solar panels to clean their water. Doctors there believe the decrease in typhoid fever is the result of more people drinking clean water. Cleaning water with solar panels means there are no plastic water bottles to worry about. But the solar panels must be placed in direct sunlight. They will not work when it's cloudy.

Many different methods have been used to increase the supply of drinkable water. Throughout the world, people need water. And as the world's population continues to grow, the demand for water will also increase. Perhaps one day water-harvesting machines and other great ideas for cleaning water will provide safe drinking water for all people around the globe.

Glossary

bacteria: Tiny living things that exist in water and air and on and inside your body. Most bacteria are helpful, but some can cause illnesses.

cholera: A disease caused by bacteria. It causes violent diarrhea and vomiting and can lead to death.

continent: One of the Earth's main land-masses. There are seven continents on the Earth.

dehydrated: When a human or animal does not have enough water in its system to maintain health.

dew point: The temperature at which condensation occurs.

diarrhea: Frequent and runny solid waste from the bowels.

generator: Machines that produce electricity. These are used for backup power when the electricity goes out.

humid: Having a lot of moisture, or water, in the air.

Humvee: A rugged vehicle used by the U.S. Army for many purposes, such as moving soldiers and supplies or launching antitank missiles.

impurities: Tiny bits of unclean material, such as dust and pollen, that are in the air.

parasites: Animals that get their food by living on or inside another animal.

polluted: Unclean.

relief organization: Any group that brings food, medicine, and other needed supplies to people suffering from natural disasters and warfare.

sewage: Liquid and solid waste from humans and animals.

technology: The use of science to make special equipment or machines.

temperature: A measure of how hot or cold things get, such as the air.

tsunami: A series of huge sea waves caused by disturbance of the ocean floor or by seismic activity.

typhoid fever: A serious and contagious disease that's caused by germs in dirty food or water.

For More Information

Web Sites

Air2Water (www.air2water.net/about_technology.html). This page of the Air2Water Web site explains the technology behind removing moisture from the air to produce drinkable water.

Air-Water Corporation (www.airwatercorp.com/). The Air-Water Corporation manufactures the AW1000M, which is used by the Red Cross. This Web site explains how their water harvester works.

Aqua Sciences, Inc. (http://aquasciences.com/). This Web site has lots of information, as well as links to news coverage, about the company's breakthrough water-harvesting machine.

Drinking Water and Ground Water Kids' Stuff, EPA (www.epa.gov/OGWDW/kids/water_trivia_facts.html). This Web site offers fun facts, games, and activities related to water, including a word scramble, matching games, and frequently asked questions.

Mirage Water Maker (www.miragewatermaker.com/). This Web site explains how the Mirage Water Maker creates drinkable water from the air.

Utah Cloud Seeding Home Page (www.water.utah.gov/cloudseeding/). This Web site run by the state government of Utah provides lots of interesting information about how cloud seeding works.

Water Related Environmental Public Health (www.cdc.gov/nceh/ehhe/water/). This section of the Centers for Disease Control and Prevention Web site offers many links to topics about the relation-ship between human health and safe drinking water.

Water, Sanitation, and Health (www.who.int/water_sanitation_health/en/). This section of the World Health Organization's Web site offers information and links concerning water quality, sanitation, and hygiene.

 **Index**

Picture Credits

About the Author

Cherese Cartlidge holds a bachelor's degree in psychology and a master's degree in middle school education. She currently works as a freelance writer and editor. Cartlidge has written several books for young people. She is a former teacher who loves being around children so much that she has two of her very own, Thomas and Liv. When she is not writing, editing, or substitute teaching, she loves to take long walks in the park with her 96-pound rottweiler puppy.